A Robbie Reader

What's So Great About...?

SAM HOUSTON

Susan Sales Harkins and
William H. Harkins

Mitchell Lane
PUBLISHERS

P.O. Box 196
Hockessin, Delaware 19707
Visit us on the web: www.mitchelllane.com
Comments? email us: mitchelllane@mitchelllane.com

Printing   1   2   3   4   5   6   7   8   9

A Robbie Reader/What's So Great About . . . ?

Annie Oakley	Daniel Boone	Davy Crockett
Ferdinand Magellan	Francis Scott Key	Henry Hudson
Jacques Cartier	Johnny Appleseed	Robert Fulton
Sam Houston		

Library of Congress Cataloging-in-Publication Data
Harkins, Susan Sales.
   Sam Houston / by Susan and William Harkins.
      p. cm. — (A Robbie Reader. What's so great about . . . ?)
   Includes bibliographical references and index.
   ISBN 1-58415-482-9 (library bound)
   1. Houston, Sam, 1793–1863—Juvenile literature. 2. United States. Congress. Senate—Biography—Juvenile literature. 3. Governors—Texas—Biography—Juvenile literature. 4. Legislators—United States—Biography—Juvenile literature. 5. Texas—History—To 1846—Juvenile literature. I. Harkins, William H. II. Title. III. Series.
   F390.H84H37 2006
   976.4'04092—dc22

                                      2005036705

ISBN-10: 1-58415-482-9   ISBN-13: 9781584154822

ABOUT THE AUTHORS: Susan and **Bill Harkins** live in Kentucky, where they enjoy writing together for children. Susan has written many books for adults and children. Bill is a history buff. In addition to writing, Bill is a member of the Kentucky National Guard.

PHOTO CREDITS: Cover—Stock Montage/Getty Images; pp. 1, 3—Sandi Winklespecht; p. 4—Bettman/CORBIS; p. 7—Horseshoe Bend National Park Museum; pp. 8, 24—North Wind Picture Archives; pp. 11, 15, 16, 23—Sharon Beck; p. 12—Hulton Archive/Getty Images; pp. 14, 18, 20, 27—Library of Congress.

PUBLISHER'S NOTE: The following story has been thoroughly researched and to the best of our knowledge represents a true story. While every possible effort has been made to ensure accuracy, the publisher will not assume liability for damages caused by inaccuracies in the data, and makes no warranty on the accuracy of the information contained herein.

                                                PLB

TABLE OF CONTENTS

Words in **bold** type can be found in the glossary.

Sam Houston enlisted in the army when he was 20 years old. He fought alongside General Andrew Jackson in the War of 1812.

A War Hero

Sam Houston watched soldiers parade up and down the street. It was March 1813, and the United States was at war with England. Sam was twenty years old and looking for work. He liked the bright uniforms the soldiers wore, so he joined the army.

When Sam told his mother that he had enlisted, she gave him a musket and a silver ring. Engraved inside the ring was the word *Honor.*

"My door is open to brave men, but my door is closed to cowards," she told him.

Sam remembered his mother's words. He became a dedicated soldier and a strong leader.

In February 1814, Sam met General Andrew Jackson. They became good friends. Cherokee Indians helped Jackson's army attack the Creek Indians. The Creeks had joined the war on Britain's side.

Sam's unit charged the Creek's small fort at Horseshoe Bend in Alabama. An arrow pierced Sam's leg. He fell to the ground in pain. Soldiers ran around him and into the fort. Sam tried to remove the arrow, but he couldn't. Another soldier stopped to help, but he couldn't pull out the arrow, either.

"Pull it out or I'll knock you to the ground!" yelled Sam over the gunfire and shouting.

The soldier tried again, and the sharp, barbed arrow tore loose in a gush of blood. A doctor dressed the wound. General Jackson ordered Sam to rest. Instead, Sam grabbed his musket and led another charge. The Creeks shot him again, twice in the right shoulder. Sam's men dragged him out of the fort.

United States soldiers and the Cherokee Indians fought the British and the Creek Indians at the Battle of Horseshoe Bend. Sam Houston suffered serious wounds at this battle. He took an arrow to the leg and suffered two gunshot wounds.

The doctor offered Sam no hope, but Sam refused to die. Two months later, he returned home. His mother opened her door wide for him. He had fought bravely. Under his mother's tender care, Sam recovered.

Sam Houston preferred the bright-colored clothing of the Cherokee Indians to the drab clothing the settlers wore. After moving to Maryville, Tennessee, Sam Houston ran away from home to live with the Cherokee.

Growing Up in Tennessee

Young Sam Houston watched the covered wagons roll past his home in Virginia. Many Virginians were moving to Tennessee. He wondered about the traveling families. Often, he daydreamed about leading his own covered wagon down the trail.

Families had been rolling past his Virginia house almost every day since he was born on March 2, 1793. It seemed everyone wanted to live in Tennessee. Even Sam's father, Major Samuel Houston, wanted to move there—but the major died before he got the chance.

After his father's funeral in 1807, Sam's daydream and his father's wish came true. Sam helped lead his family's wagons down the Great

Warrior and Trading Path. The Houstons traveled 300 miles from their home near Lexington, Virginia, to Maryville, Tennessee. Their new home was just five miles north of Cherokee land.

Sam worked to make the new farm a success. Unlike his brothers, Sam hated farming. No one was surprised when one day he just disappeared. His older brothers found him living with the Cherokee. Life with the Indians was fun for Sam, so he stayed with them.

Oolooteka, the tribe's chief, was like a father to Sam. The chief adopted him and called him Kalanu (kuh-LAH-nuh), which means "the Raven" in Cherokee. Sam dressed in bright clothes and wore a large cloth around his head like the Cherokee men. He respected and loved his new Indian father.

The Cherokee taught Sam how to dance and how to play ball. He also learned how to carve wood, or whittle. Mostly, Sam loved to read, and his Indian family let him read in peace.

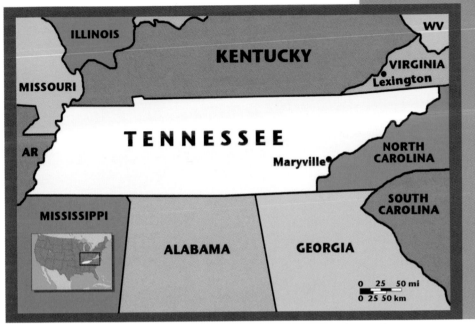

During the early 1800s many families moved west from the northeast. Sam Houston was still a child, just fourteen, when he helped his family move from Virginia to Maryville, Tennessee.

For three years, Sam lived with the Cherokee. Then he became a teacher. He wore his bright Indian clothes and headdress to school. He was a good teacher, and his students liked him.

During the War of 1812, Sam joined the army. He fought bravely and made his mother proud. The rest of his life, Sam suffered from the war wounds he received at Horseshoe Bend.

Sam Houston served as a senator and governor for the state of Tennessee. He was able to convince the Cherokee to move west to Arkansas after the War of 1812.

Cherokee Friend and U.S. Politician

After the War of 1812, the Cherokee chiefs signed a **treaty** with U.S. government agents. The chiefs agreed to move their people farther west, to Arkansas. The agents promised them new land. Also, the government would provide food and houses for the Cherokee in Arkansas.

Some Cherokee refused to go. General Jackson asked Houston to visit his Indian family. He hoped Houston could talk the Cherokee into moving. The Cherokee wondered whether Houston was their old friend or their new enemy.

Andrew Jackson helped win the War of 1812 and later became president of the United States. Although Jackson may have helped the Cherokee in 1830 by firing dishonest agents, he also signed the Indian Removal Act that year. As a result, about 4,000 Cherokee would die from their forced march to Oklahoma in 1838.

They didn't wonder for long. Houston was mad when he learned the government agents had not kept their promises. He traveled to Washington, D.C., to complain about the broken treaty. While in the capitol, Houston wore his bright Indian clothes and headdress. He wanted to show that he represented his Cherokee friends.

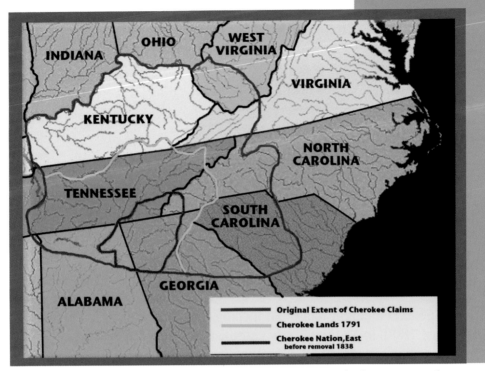

The Cherokee Indians claimed a huge territory, including parts of several states. As white settlers moved west, that territory shrank.

Houston finally convinced the Cherokee to move west. They trusted him and believed he would force the government to keep its promises. He was sad to see his friends go. He believed they would be safe and happy in Arkansas.

Houston thought that if he were a member of the government, he could make laws that

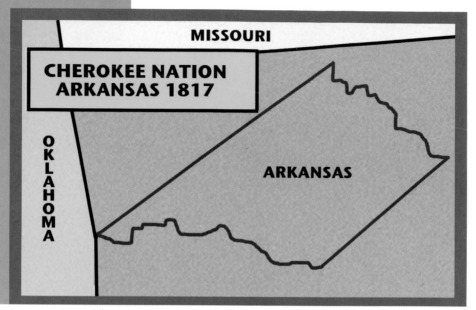

CHEROKEE NATION ARKANSAS 1817

MISSOURI

OKLAHOMA

ARKANSAS

European settlement had been forcing the Cherokee west since before 1800. In 1817, a treaty established Cherokee Nation boundaries in Arkansas. At Andrew Jackson's request, Houston convinced Chief Oolooteka and his people to move there. The Cherokee were not happy in Arkansas. The land was different and the U.S. government did not fulfill all its promises. Houston tried to help the Cherokee and met with President Jackson about the problem.

protected the Cherokee. He ran for **Congress** and was elected in 1823. A few years later, he was elected governor of Tennessee as well.

The people of Tennessee thought a lot of Sam until tragedy struck. In April 1829, Sam's young wife, Eliza, left him. They had been married for only a few months. Houston's enemies said that he must have been a bad husband. The breakup caused a terrible **scandal**. Houston quit his job as governor.

For a long time, Houston was sad and lonely. He visited Oolooteka in Arkansas. Spending time with his Cherokee family helped. The Cherokee nation adopted him as a brother.

In 1830, Houston traveled to Washington, D.C., to visit his old friend Andrew Jackson. Jackson was now the president of the United States. Houston complained about the government agents who had cheated the Cherokee. President Jackson listened to Houston. He didn't like what his friend told him. He fired some of the dishonest agents.

During that visit, President Jackson talked to Houston about the Texas **territory**. He hoped that someday Texas would become a state. He needed Houston's help to make that dream come true. Houston said he would go to Texas to help.

Stephen Austin is known as the Father of Texas. Austin, the capital city of Texas, is named for him.

The Fight for Texas

Sam Houston arrived in Texas in December 1832. At that time, Texas belonged to Mexico. While traveling through the territory, Houston met with Jim Bowie, a friend from the War of 1812. Bowie owned a lot of land in Texas. Houston also met Stephen F. Austin, who had established the first American colony in Texas, and William B. Travis, a lawyer for the colonists. Houston learned from these men that most **Texians** wanted Texas to be an independent country.

Houston and a few other Texians met to write a **constitution** for a free Texas. That made the Mexican government mad. Texas belonged to Mexico! Austin, who had carried the

William Travis was a lawyer and soldier. He led the Texas forces at the Battle of the Alamo.

constitution to Mexico, was put in jail (until Sept. 1, 1835). General Antonio López de Santa Anna, Mexico's president, sent several thousand soldiers to Texas.

About 188 men, including Bowie and Austin, fought the Mexican soldiers at the **Alamo**. Texians asked Houston to bring help to the men at the small fort. Before help could arrive, the Mexican army had killed everyone inside.

General Santa Anna commanded a huge army. If Sam Houston had not tricked him, Texas probably wouldn't have won the revolution for independence.

The Texians insisted that Houston attack Santa Anna's army. Houston decided to trick Santa Anna instead. There were more Mexican soldiers than Texian soldiers. Houston would have to be smarter than Santa Anna to win Texas.

On April 21, 1836, twenty-five hundred Mexican soldiers camped near the San Jacinto River. Since it was a hot afternoon, they rested. Many took a **siesta**. While they slept, Houston's 743 men crept up to the camp.

21

Santa Anna (with red shawl) surrendered to Sam Houston (lying down) after losing the Battle of San Jacinto. The Mexican general had tried to escape to Mexico by changing his uniform for street clothes. Houston was wounded, but was well enough to accept the general's surrender. Eventually, Houston let Santa Anna return to Mexico.

"Remember the Alamo!" Houston cried as they ran toward the sleeping soldiers.

The Mexicans were surprised. Many deserted in the confusion. The battle lasted only eighteen minutes. Because of Houston's plan, fewer than ten Texians died that day. In the fight, a bullet broke Houston's ankle. The Mexicans suffered many losses. The Texians

Texians fought for independence from Mexico in 1835 and 1836. Santa Anna's forces triumphed at the Alamo on March 6, 1836. They surrendered to Houston six weeks later at San Jacinto.

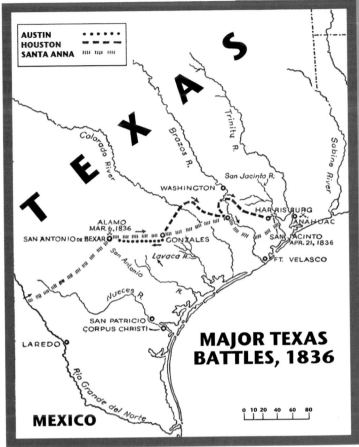

MAJOR TEXAS BATTLES, 1836

killed, wounded, or captured 1,500 Mexican soldiers.

The Texians caught Santa Anna before he could escape to Mexico. He surrendered Texas to Sam Houston and the Texians. Grateful Texians elected Houston the first president of the Republic of Texas.

Sam Houston's capture of Santa Anna made him a hero throughout the Texas territory. He served as the first president of the Republic of Texas. Later, he served as governor and senator for the state of Texas.

Texas!

Houston spent the next two years helping Texas get a strong start as a **republic**. He worked hard as president, and Texians respected him. Still, Houston hoped that Texas would join the United States someday.

After Houston left the presidency in 1838, he traveled. In Alabama, he fell in love with Margaret Moffett Lea. She was just twenty and Sam was forty-seven. People thought he was too old for her. Margaret disagreed, and she married Sam on May 9, 1840.

Houston saw his wish come true when Texas became a state in 1846. Texans remembered Sam and sent him to Washington, D.C., as a senator. He missed Margaret and his children. When he wasn't working, he sat on the porch and whittled toys.

He listened to his friends argue about slavery. People in the north wanted to **abolish** it. Many in the south wanted to keep their slaves. Houston knew that many Texans owned slaves. Some even wanted to **secede** from the **Union**. Houston wanted Texas to remain a state.

Houston was the governor of Texas in 1861 when Abraham Lincoln became president of the United States. The United States was facing a **civil** war. Southern slave owners did not trust Lincoln. Angry Texans voted to secede and fight Lincoln. Houston wanted Texas to remain in the Union, so he resigned as governor of Texas. The war began on April 12.

Two years later, the North and South were still fighting. Houston couldn't fight in the war. He was too old and sick. On July 26, 1863, Margaret sat by Sam's bed and held his hand while he slept. For just a moment, he woke up.

"Texas. Texas. Margaret," said Houston weakly, and then he died.

Abraham Lincoln took office as the president of the United States in 1861. The country was in turmoil over the issue of slavery. Lincoln abolished slavery in the United States in 1863. The Civil War would last until April 1865.

Sam Houston loved the United States, and he loved Texas. He is the only man to serve as a member of congress and governor in one state (Tennessee), as a senator and governor in another state (Texas), and as president of an independent republic (Texas). He led a dangerous and exciting, but honorable, life.

27

CHRONOLOGY

1793   Sam Houston is born on March 2 to Major Sam Houston and Elizabeth Paxton Houston at Timber Ridge, Rockbridge County, in Virginia.

1807   Elizabeth Houston moves her nine children to Maryville, Tennessee.

1809   Sam runs away from home to live with the Cherokee.

1813   Houston enlists in the regular army as a private.

1814   Houston is pierced by an arrow and then shot twice at the Battle of Horseshoe Bend during the War of 1812.

1816   Houston becomes an Indian agent in Tennessee.

1818   Houston leads a group of Cherokee to Washington, D.C., to meet with Secretary of War John Calhoun.

1823   Houston is elected to the U.S. House of Representatives.

1827   Houston is elected governor of Tennessee.

1829   Houston marries Eliza Allen on January 22.
Sam and Eliza separate on April 9.
Houston resigns as governor of Tennessee on April 16.
Houston visits his Indian father, Chief Oolooteka, in Arkansas in May.
Houston becomes a Cherokee citizen in October.

1830   Houston discusses Indian issues with Andrew Jackson in Washington, D.C.

1832   Houston travels to Texas on a special mission for President Andrew Jackson.

1836   Houston attends the Texas Constitutional Convention on March 1 and takes command of the Texas Army on March 4.
Houston learns that the Mexican Army has defeated the Texians at the Alamo (March 6).

Houston's army attacks Santa Anna at San Jacinto on April 21.
Santa Anna signs a treaty of surrender on April 22.
Houston is elected president of the Republic of Texas on September 5.

1838 Houston leaves the presidency in December.

1840 Houston marries Margaret Lea.

1841 Houston is reelected as president of Texas.

1845 Texas is admitted as a state to the United States in December.

1846 Houston becomes a U.S. Senator for Texas.

1859 Houston becomes governor of Texas in December.

1861 The state of Texas secedes from the Union on March 4.
Houston does not want Texas to join the Confederate states; he resigns as governor on March 16.
The Civil War begins on April 12.

1863 Houston dies of pneumonia on July 26.

FIND OUT MORE

Books

Boraas, Tracey. *Sam Houston: Soldier and Statesman.* Mankato, Minnesota: Bridgestone Books, 2002.

Gregson, Susan R. *Sam Houston: Texas Hero.* Minneapolis: Compass Point Books, 2006.

Sanford, William R., and Carl R. Green. *Sam Houston: Texas Hero.* Berkeley Heights, New Jersey: Enslow Publishers, Inc., 1996.

Trumbauer, Lisa. *Sam Houston*. Mankato, Minnesota: Pebble
  Books, 2003.
Wade, Mary Dodson. *I Am Houston*. Houston, Texas:
  Colophon House, 1993.

Works Consulted

De Bruhl, Marshall. *Sword of San Jacinto: A Life of Sam
  Houston*. New York: Random House, 1993.
Haley, James L. *Sam Houston*. Norman, Oklahoma: University
  of Oklahoma Press, 2002.
Houston, Sam, Donald Day, and Harry Herbert Ullom. *The
  Autobiography of Sam Houston*. Norman, Oklahoma:
  University of Oklahoma Press, 1954.
James, Marquis. *The Raven: A Biography of Sam Houston*.
  New York: Blue Ribbon Books, Inc., 1929.
Mooney, Booth. *Sam Houston*. Follett Publishing Company,
  1965.
Williams, John Hoyt. *Sam Houston: A Biography of the Father
  of Texas*. New York: Simon & Schuster, 1993.

On the Internet

American Experience: Remember the Alamo
  http://www.pbs.org/wgbh/amex/alamo/
The Alamo
  http://www.thealamo.org/
The Sam Houston Memorial Museum
  http://www.samhouston.org/
Texas, the Lone Star State
  http://www.kidskonnect.com/Texas/TexasHome.html

GLOSSARY

abolish (ah-BAH-lish)—To do away with completely.

Alamo (AA-luh-moh)—A mission, or church, that was used as a fort in southern Texas.

civil (SIH-vul)—Relating to citizens, and not the military.

Congress (KON-gris)—Representatives of the people to the government.

constitution (kon-stih-TOO-shen)—Laws of the government.

republic (ree-PUB-lik)—An independent territory or nation that is governed by a president and whose citizens have the right to vote.

scandal (SKAN-dul)—A disgraceful incident that harms a person's reputation.

secede (seh-SEED)—To leave a group.

siesta (see-ES-tah)—Mexican word for "nap," usually taken after lunch.

territory (TAYR-ih-tor-ee)—An area of land that shares a government, such as parts of North America before they were made states.

Texian (TEK-see-in)—A person who lived in Texas before it became a republic.

treaty (TREE-tee)—An agreement that settles a conflict.

Union (YOON-yun)—Another name for the United States during the Civil War. The southern states that seceded were not part of the Union. They joined together to form the Confederate States of America.

INDEX